Catholic Prayers
for the Separated and Divorced

Catholic Prayer Book

for the Separated and Divorced

Woodeene Koenig-Bricker
and
David Dziena

Our Sunday Visitor Publishing Division
Our Sunday Visitor, Inc.
Huntington, Indiana 46750

Nihil Obstat
Msgr. Michael Heintz, Ph.D.
Censor Librorum

Imprimatur
✠ Kevin C. Rhoades
Bishop of Fort Wayne-South Bend
October 7, 2014

The *Nihil Obstat* and *Imprimatur* are official declarations that a book is free from doctrinal or moral error. It is not implied that those who have granted the *Nihil Obstat* and *Imprimatur* agree with the contents, opinions, or statements expressed.

Scripture texts in this work, except where noted, are taken from the *New American Bible, revised edition* © 2010, 1991, 1986, 1970 Confraternity of Christian Doctrine, Washington, D.C., and are used by permission of the copyright owner. All rights reserved. No part of the *New American Bible* may be reproduced in any form without permission in writing from the copyright owner.

The English translation of Act of Contrition from *Rite of Penance* © 1974 International Commission on English in the Liturgy Corporation (ICEL); the English translation of the Apostles' Creed from The *Roman Missal* © 2010. All rights reserved.

Every reasonable effort has been made to determine copyright holders of excerpted materials and to secure permissions as needed. If any copyrighted materials have been inadvertently used in this work without proper credit being given in one form or another, please notify Our Sunday Visitor in writing.

ISBN: 978-1-61278-838-8 (Inventory No. T1644)
eISBN: 978-1-61278-841-8
LCCN: 2014949422

Cover design: Amanda Falk
Cover art: Shutterstock
Interior design: Maggie Urgo
PRINTED IN THE UNITED STATES OF AMERICA

From Woodeene
For my son, Matthew

From David
For my children, Timothy, Geoffrey, Anya,
and Dominick, and my stepchildren,
Michael and Matthew

Table of Contents

Preface

"Dear brothers and sisters, let us not be closed to the newness that God wants to bring into our lives! Are we often weary, disheartened, and sad? Do we feel weighted down by our sins? Do we think that we won't be able to cope? Let us not close our hearts, let us not lose confidence, let us never give up: there are no situations which God cannot change, there is no sin which he cannot forgive if only we open ourselves to him."

— *Pope Francis, Homily, Easter Vigil, March 30, 2013*

The sad reality is that many Catholic marriages fail and even good Catholics get divorced. When that happens, all too often, the people involved not only have to go through the difficulties of the divorce itself, but they can feel isolated and removed from the faith as well. In a time when they need the comfort and encouragement of their community, they can feel isolated and abandoned by the Church.

Pope Saint John Paul II wrote in *Familiaris Consortio*, "I earnestly call upon pastors and the whole community of the faithful to help the divorced, and with solicitous care to make sure that they do not consider themselves as separated from the Church, for as baptized persons they can, and indeed must, share in her life" (No. 84).

Pope Francis has taken up this call in the synod that focused on the pastoral challenges of the family, with a special emphasis on divorced and remarried Catholics, as well as those who are living in painful and unresolved situations.

Inspired by this, we have created a book of short prayers that we hope will help you if you are faced with the end of a marriage, an annulment, and perhaps a remarriage. Both of us have gone through the pain of divorce and know the pain and challenges in our own lives.

It is our prayer that you will find acceptance and peace in these reflections as well as the courage to rebuild your life with the grace and guidance of the Holy Spirit.

Part I: *Prayers for the Five Stages of Loss and Grief*

"The only people who think there's a time limit for grief have never lost a piece of their heart. Take all the time you need."
— *Unknown*

We all know that people go through certain universal stages of grief after a death, but we go through these same stages after any significant loss — including a divorce.

While the stages are often listed in the order below, they don't necessarily occur this way for all people. In fact, you might not even go through all of them, or you may pass quickly through one stage but find yourself remaining in another for weeks or even months. And don't be surprised if you find yourself revisiting a stage you thought you had finished. We often go back and forth between stages until we finally reach a place of peace and acceptance.

The value of the stages of grief is that they can help you understand that your feelings are normal, and that they will get better over time. This, in turn, can help you have patience with yourself as you adapt to your new life situation.

1. Denial and Isolation
You may be tempted to not even want to think about what is happening and to hide from anyone who wants

to discuss it. This is a normal reaction to the shock and pain of the reality of the end of a marriage.

2. Anger

Anger is very common, especially if infidelity has been involved. We may be angry at our former spouse, angry at friends and family who have taken sides, and even angry at ourselves. We may lash out at our children, our friends, even our pets.

3. Bargaining

While honest prayer is answered, bargaining is an attempt to manipulate God into giving you your will. In particular, if you aren't the one who wanted the divorce, trying to strike a deal with God to save the marriage often occurs. The other side of bargaining is self-doubt and recrimination: If only I had spent less time on my hobbies… Both forms of bargaining are part of the normal stages of grieving.

4. Depression

This stage is what we usually call "sadness." It's a deep-seated sense of pain and loss, sometimes accompanied by a lack of interest in life and a withdrawal from activities. While normal, if this type of depression lasts more than a few months after a divorce, consider getting some professional counseling.

5. Acceptance

This is the final stage of coping with the loss and death of a marriage. Don't confuse it with "being happy again." It's merely the place where you make peace with what has happened and begin to prepare to move on. For Catholics, the annulment process can be a great help in reaching this place of healing.

Denial and Isolation

My God, my God, why have you forsaken me?
   Why are you so far from saving me,
   so far from my cries of anguish?
My God, I cry out by day, but you do not answer,
   by night, but I find no rest.

— Psalms 22:1-2, NIV

My God, at times I think I will wake up and it
   will all have been a bad dream. I can hardly
   believe that my marriage has ended or that my
   pleas for a different outcome seem to have gone
   unanswered.

I feel so alone. I feel like an abandoned child.

Lord, you know how much this hurts. You know
   how the pain of divorce is with me day and
   night. You know how disappointed I am that my
   marriage failed and how sad I am that it came
   to this.

But I also know that even in the midst of this you
   still love me and will be with me. Please show
   me your presence and grant me your comfort so
   that I might someday have the courage to hope
   again. Amen.

---

*Meditate on the crucifix and remember that Christ
knows what it is like to feel as though the Father
doesn't hear your cries or understand your pain. Allow Christ to join you in your pain.*

Anger

"There must be no hostility in our minds, no contempt in our eyes, no insult on our lips."

— Saint John Bosco

Jesus, the feeling of anger burns within my heart. It threatens to take over my life and tempts me to say and do things that I know I will regret.

Help me to accept the fact that anger is a part of grief, but do not let me sin in my anger.

Guard my tongue and guard my heart, that I may get through this stage of grief with grace and courage.

And, dear Jesus, help me to remember that my former spouse may be feeling anger toward me as well. Let me not react to his/her anger with more anger, and do not let my actions create even more discord between us.

Please, Lord, cover our lives with your peace. Amen.

Read Ephesians 4:26-27. Forgive your former spouse — and forgive yourself — for anything you might have said or done in anger.

Bargaining

"Ask and it will be given you; seek and you will find; knock and the door will be opened to you. For everyone who asks, receives; and the one who seeks, finds; and to the one who knocks, the door will be opened."

— Matthew 7:7-8

My Lord, I don't really know what I want except
   that I want you to fix this.
Maybe you can restore my marriage and bring my
   spouse and me back into a loving relationship
   with each other?
Or maybe you can just get it over with as quickly
   as possible?
All I know is that I want to do what is best in this
   difficult situation.
Be with me — and with my former spouse — that
   we both may be open to your will for our lives,
   whatever that might be.
I know that all things are possible with you, even
   those things that seem utterly impossible to me.
Above all, God, I ask that you give me the courage
   to continue to seek your face, no matter what
   happens next. Amen.

Do you ask God for what you need, or do you bargain with him? Be direct with God, even if it is embarrassing, uncomfortable, or difficult. He will answer your prayers in his time and in his way. Be open to it.

Depression

"I know God will not give me anything I can't handle. I just wish he didn't trust me so much."

— Attributed to Blessed Teresa of Calcutta

Dear God, I feel like I'm submerged in darkness, like I will never have another bright, happy day in my life. I try to appear cheerful and hopeful for my family, especially my children, but inside I am empty.

I cry out to you, but I hear nothing but the silence of my own sorrow. God, why do you not answer me?

With the ending of my marriage, I feel like a failure, worthless, useless. Yet, despite it, I choose to believe that you are here with me in my depression. I choose to believe that you will not abandon me to my feelings, but will give me the courage and the hope that things can and will get better.

Be with me, my God. I need you now more than I have ever needed you. Amen.

Feelings of abandonment, anger, embarrassment, loneliness, and despair are just some of the paths that lead us to depression. Do not allow yourself to believe that God has abandoned you. Pray for the strength to overcome depression, and seek help when you think you can't.

Acceptance

"Bad things do happen; how I respond to them defines my character and the quality of my life. I can choose to sit in perpetual sadness, immobilized by the gravity of my loss, or I can choose to rise from the pain and treasure the most precious gift I have — life itself."

— *Walter Anderson*

Serenity Prayer
By Reinhold Niebuhr

God, give me grace to accept with serenity
the things that cannot be changed,
Courage to change the things
which should be changed,
and the Wisdom to distinguish
the one from the other.
Living one day at a time,
Enjoying one moment at a time,
Accepting hardship as a pathway to peace,
Taking, as Jesus did, this sinful world as it is, not as
I would have it,
Trusting that You will make all things right,
if I surrender to Your will,
So that I may be reasonably happy in this life,
and supremely happy with You forever in the next.
Amen.

Pray for the grace to accept the good and bad in your life, and the courage to learn and grow from it.

Part II: *Prayers for My Children*

"*To maintain a joyful family requires much from both the parents and the children. Each member of the family has to become, in a special way, the servant of the others.*"

— *Pope Saint John Paul II*

For My Kids

"When mom and dad went to war the only prisoners they took were the children."

— *Pat Conroy*

Dear God, you know how much I love my
   children.
Grant me your own heart so that I might always
   be there for my children,
no matter if we are together or if we are apart.
Let them know that my love for them will never
   waver, never end,
no matter what is happening between me and their
   mother/father.
Do not let the hard feelings that divorce creates
   ever cause them to doubt my love for them.
Help me to keep their needs as my highest priority,
   and give me the courage to make whatever
   sacrifices are needed to ensure that they always
   feel loved.
I ask this, as your own child, trusting in your love
   for me. Amen.

---

*What can you do to keep your child/children out
of any disagreements you have with your former
spouse? Make a daily commitment to do what you
can to shield them from the ugliness that can come
from a separation or divorce. Put their well-being
first.*

Guardian Angel Prayer
to Watch Over My Children

"For he commands his angels with regard to you, / to guard you wherever you go."
— Psalms 91:11

My dear Guardian Angel, I know that you have
    watched over me since my birth. Now I ask that
    you watch over my children as well,
    especially when I cannot be with them.
Let them know that they are always in my heart,
    no matter where we are,
    and that I am no further than a prayer away.
Guide them, today and always.
Protect them, today and always.
Watch over them, today and always.
Amen.

Not seeing your children daily is one of the most painful results of a separation or divorce. Trust that God will protect them and keep them safe, even when they are not in your care. Think of ways he can help you cope with the void you feel in your heart when they are not with you.

For My Stepchildren

"Parenthood requires love, not DNA."

— Unknown

God, you have brought these children into my life.
They are not bone of my bone or blood of my
    blood,
but you have asked that I love and care for them.
Give me a heart that is big enough to love them
    because I love their mother/father.
Grant that I do not try to take the place of their
    other parent, but that I can be another stable,
    loving adult in their lives.
Help me to find the line between friendship and
    parenthood, so that my influence will always be
    for good.
Let me be the best stepparent I can be, so that love
    and harmony will be a part of these children's
    lives.
This I ask you, in the name of Jesus, in union with
    the Holy Spirit. Amen.

Have you felt that being a stepparent can be a thankless job? Pray for the humility required for all forms of parenting and accept that you may not be rewarded or acknowledged for the good work that you do.

For When Stepparents and Stepchildren Fight

"Stepparenting: It's just like parenting, but with none of the credit and all of the blame."

— *Unknown*

My Lord, I come before you with a torn and aching
heart.
I love my new husband/wife, and I want my
children to love him/her as well.
Yet, they always seem to be in conflict.
You know that I want everyone to be happy.
I want to solve this for them, but I know that they
have to work out their own relationships.
Help me to have the strength and grace to give
them the space they need,
while still making sure that both my spouse and
my children know how much I love them.
Let me know when to speak, and when to hold my
tongue.
Let me know what to say, and what not to say.
Most of all, help me be a model of your unending
and steadfast love for all our children. Amen.

---

*When there are disagreements with your new spouse
and your children, do you wonder if it is worth it? Do
you take the fights personally? Remember that in any
meaningful relationship there will be ups and downs.
Pray that the relationship between your new partner
and your children will improve and grow.*

For When You Don't Get Along with Your Stepchildren

"Stepparenting is a daily decision to love someone because you love their parent."

— *Anonymous*

Lord, I sometimes find it hard to love my spouse's
    children.
At times I even wish that they didn't have to be
    a part of our lives. Then I feel guilty, and that
    makes things even more difficult.
God, help me to see these children with your eyes,
to care for them as you care for them,
to love them as you love them.
Give me the gifts of understanding and
    compassion so that my relationship with my
    stepchildren does not become a source of stress
    for my marriage.
Most of all, help me to remember that love is a
    decision that I can make every day. Amen.

Is your relationship with your spouse's children putting a strain on your new marriage? Reflect on what you can do to improve your relationship with your stepchildren. Remind yourself that this can take time, and it may not end up looking like you think it should.

For Patience with My Children

"Between your child's action and your reaction, you have the space to decide how it is best to think, feel and respond. You have a choice."

— *Debbie Pincus*

Father, you know what it is like to lose patience
   with your children,
yet your loving kindness extends from generation
   to generation.
I have been the recipient of your grace and love, so
   now I ask that you help me pass that grace and
   love on to my children.
I know they are struggling with all the changes in
   our lives.
I realize that they are grieving the loss of the
   family they knew and the image they had of
   themselves.
I know that this is hard on them and that they may
   act out and misbehave because they are in pain.
Help me to take time before I react in anger or
   frustration to put myself in their place and act
   out of compassion and empathy.
Grant that I may be willing to put their needs
   before my own wants.

Any parent can lose their patience with their child. It can be even more challenging in a separation or divorce. Reflect on the times you have lost your patience with your child/children. Think about how you could do better next time.

Prayer When My Former Spouse Is Causing Scandal for My Children

"Scandal is grave when given by those who by nature or office are obliged to teach and educate others. Jesus reproaches the scribes and Pharisees on this account: he likens them to wolves in sheep's clothing."

— Catechism of the Catholic Church, *2285*

Oh God, I can't believe what my former husband/wife is doing!

His/her actions go against everything that I want my children to do and be. I don't want them to hate their mother/father, but I need your wisdom to know how to explain to them that we can "hate the sin" but "love the sinner."

Holy Spirit, guard my tongue that I may explain what is wrong without creating more discord. Especially help me not to speak ill about their parent when we talk about this situation.

And if you see fit to allow me to talk to my former spouse about his/her actions, help me to do so without being hostile or accusatory but with compassion and grace.

I ask this in the name of the Father, the Son and the Holy Spirit. Amen

---

It is especially sad when a parent causes scandal or sets a poor example for a child. Pray to the Holy Spirit that you may speak the compassionate truth when you speak with your child about the scandal caused by others.

Prayer for Peaceful Interaction with My Former Spouse

"We are both beautiful and great people who just happen to bring out the ugly in one another at times."
— *Unknown*

Jesus, Son of David, have mercy on me.
Help me to reconcile with my former spouse
    insofar as we are able
so that your peace, which passes all understanding,
    can be present in all our dealings.
The next time we must talk, grant me the ability
    to speak without rancor, and help us to come
    to mutually beneficial agreements, especially
    where our children are concerned.
As we speak, bring to mind the love we once
    shared and let that memory fill our
    conversations with compassion.
Most of all, Lord, guard me from reacting with
    anger no matter what is said.
May I be a true witness of Christian peace and love
    in all I say and do toward my former spouse.

Because of your children, your former spouse will be in your life forever. It can be challenging to have a civil conversation with someone that you no longer love in the same way as when you were married. Think about how you can be a peacemaker, even in the face of hatred. Pray that you can be steadfast in this essential quality of a Christian.

Blessing for Children Departing for the Other Parent's Home

"The one thing that matters more than anything else today is the quality of your relationships."

— *Wesley Furlong*

Father, be with (insert name) as he/she goes to be
with his/her other parent.
Bless their time together and give them peace and
joy.
This we ask in the name of the Father, Son and
Holy Spirit. *(Make Sign of the Cross and repeat
with each child.)*

---

*Being apart from your children can be painful. It is
the casualty of most divorces. Pray for the ability to be
present, both emotionally and physically, when your
children are with you. Remind them that you love
and miss them even when they are not with you. Reflect on your recent time with them and use the time
apart as a chance to "reload" and be an even better
parent the next time they are with you.*

Part III: *Traditional Prayers and Devotions*

"*Prayer is the best weapon we possess, the key that opens the heart of God.*"

— *Saint Padre Pio*

Making a Spiritual Communion When I Cannot Receive Communion

"I earnestly call upon pastors and the whole community of the faithful to help the divorced, and with solicitous care to make sure that they do not consider themselves as separated from the Church, for as baptized persons they can, and indeed must, share in her life."

— *Saint John Paul II* (Familiaris Consortio, 84)

My Jesus,
I believe that you are in the Blessed Sacrament.
I love you above all things, and I long for you in
    my soul.
Since I cannot now receive you sacramentally,
come at least spiritually into my heart.
As though you have already come,
I embrace you and unite myself entirely to you;
never permit me to be separated from you.
Amen.

— *Saint Alphonsus Liguori*

If you are divorced but not remarried, you are still a member of the Church and can receive the sacraments, including the Eucharist. Only if you have remarried without an annulment are you asked to refrain from receiving Communion. Contact your pastor to discuss the particulars of your situation so you can once again receive Eucharistic Communion. For more information on divorced but not remarried Catholics read the Catechism, 2386. For those remarried outside of the Church, refer to 1665.

The Lord's Prayer

"Stop judging and you will not be judged. Stop condemning and you will not be condemned. Forgive and you will be forgiven."

— *Luke 6:37*

Our Father, who art in heaven,
hallowed be thy name;
thy kingdom come;
thy will be done
on earth as it is in heaven.
Give us this day our daily bread;
and forgive us our trespasses
as we forgive those
who trespass against us;
and lead us not into temptation,
but deliver us from evil.
Amen.

What do you need God to help you with? Who do you need to forgive? How can God protect you from evil?

The Apostles' Creed

"Creeds do not say merely what we believe, but what is. Creeds wake us from our dreams and prejudices into objective reality. Creeds do not confine us in little cages, as the modern world thinks; creeds free us into the outdoors, into the real world where the winds of heaven whip around our heads."

— Peter Kreeft

I believe in God,
the Father Almighty,
Creator of Heaven and earth;
and in Jesus Christ, his only Son, our Lord,
who was conceived by the Holy Spirit,
born of the Virgin Mary,
suffered under Pontius Pilate,
was crucified, died and was buried;
he descended into hell;
on the third day he arose again from the dead;
he ascended into heaven,
and is seated at the right hand of God the Father
    almighty;
from there he will come to judge the living and the
    dead.
I believe in the Holy Spirit,
the holy Catholic Church,
the communion of saints,
the forgiveness of sins,
the resurrection of the body,
and the life everlasting. Amen.

Pray this ancient prayer with conviction and joy to declare your decision to live as a Christian.

Glory Be

"Praise God, from whom all blessings flow;
Praise him, all creatures here below;
Praise him above, ye heavenly host;
Praise Father, Son, and Holy Ghost."
    — *Thomas Ken, "Awake, My Soul, and with the Sun"*

Glory be to the Father,
and to the Son,
and to the Holy Spirit.
As it was in the beginning,
is now, and ever shall be,
world without end. Amen.

In good moments or bad moments, offer this prayer
of praise to surrender all to God and to acknowledge
his goodness to you.

Prayers to the Holy Spirit

"If you love me, you will keep my commandments. And I will ask the Father, and he will give you another Advocate to be with you always, the Spirit of truth, which the world cannot accept, because it neither sees nor knows it. But you know it, because it remains with you, and will be in you."

— *John 14:15-17*

Come, Holy Spirit

Come Holy Spirit, fill the hearts of your faithful
and kindle in them the fire of your love.
Send forth your Spirit and they shall be created.
And You shall renew the face of the earth.

Let us pray.
O, God, who by the light of the Holy Spirit, did
instruct the hearts of the faithful, grant that by
the same Holy Spirit we may be truly wise and
ever enjoy His consolations, through Christ Our
Lord. Amen.

Veni Creator Spiritus

O Holy Spirit by whose breath
Life rises vibrant out of death:
Come to create, renew, inspire;
Come, kindle in our hearts your fire.

You are the seekers sure resource,
Of burning love the living source,
Protector in the midst of strife,
The giver and the Lord of life.

In you God's energy is shown,
To us your varied gifts made known.
Teach us to speak, teach us to hear;
Yours is the tongue and yours the ear.

Flood our dull senses with your light;
In mutual love our hearts unite.
Your power the whole creation fills;
Confirm our weak, uncertain wills.

From inner strife grant us release;
Turn nations to the ways of peace.
To fuller life your people bring
That as one body we may sing:

Praise to the Father, Christ his Word,
And to the Spirit, God the Lord:
To them all honor, glory be
Both now and in eternity. Amen.

Remember that the Holy Spirit is your Advocate. That means he is your Defender, your Counselor, your Protector, your Comforter, and more. So when you pray to him, entrust all your concerns to him and expect him to act.

Prayers to Mary

"If you ever feel distressed during your day — call upon Our Lady — just say this simple prayer: 'Mary, Mother of Jesus, please be a mother to me now.' I must admit — this prayer has never failed me."

— *Blessed Mother Teresa*

Hail Mary

Hail Mary, full of grace,
the Lord is with thee.
Blessed art thou among women,
and blessed is the fruit of thy womb, Jesus.
Holy Mary, Mother of God,
pray for us sinners,
now and at the hour of our death.
Amen.

Hail, Holy Queen

Hail, holy Queen, Mother of mercy. Hail, our life, our sweetness and our hope. To thee do we cry, poor banished children of Eve. To thee do we send up our sighs, mourning and weeping in this vale of tears. Turn then, most gracious Advocate, thine eyes of mercy toward us, and after this, our exile, show unto us the blessed fruit of thy womb, Jesus. O clement, O loving, O sweet Virgin Mary! Amen.

The Memorare

Remember, O most gracious Virgin Mary, that never was it known that anyone who fled to thy protection, implored thy help, or sought thine intercession was left unaided.

Inspired by this confidence, I fly unto thee, O Virgin of virgins, my mother; to thee do I come, before thee I stand, sinful and sorrowful. O Mother of the Word Incarnate, despise not my petitions, but in thy mercy, hear and answer me. Amen.

Do you honor Mary as your Mother? What can she help you with? Pray through Mary to Jesus. She will help you. "In the difficult moments of life, Christians can turn to the Mother of God and find protection and care," says Pope Francis.

Rosary for the Separated and Divorced

"You have heard that it was said, 'You shall love your neighbor and hate your enemy.' But I say to you, love your enemies, and pray for those who persecute you, that you may be children of your heavenly Father, for he makes his sun rise on the bad and the good, and causes rain to fall on the just and the unjust. For if you love those who love you, what recompense will you have? Do not the tax collectors do the same? And if you greet your brothers only, what is unusual about that? Do not the pagans do the same? So be perfect, just as your heavenly Father is perfect."

— *Matthew 5:43-48*

How to Pray the Rosary

1. Pray the Sign of the Cross and the Apostles' Creed
2. Pray the Lord's Prayer.
3. Pray three Hail Marys.
4. Pray the Glory Be.
5. Say the first mystery; then pray the Lord's Prayer.
6. Pray 10 Hail Marys while meditating on the mystery.
7. Pray the Glory Be.
8. Say the second mystery; then pray the Lord's Prayer. (Repeat steps 6 and 7 and continue with the third, fourth, and fifth mysteries of the day in the same manner.)
9. Pray the Hail, Holy Queen.

For more information, visit www.osv.com/Portals/4/documents/pdf/howtorosary.pdf

Joyful Mysteries
(Monday and Saturday)
1. The Annunciation
2. The Visitation
3. The Birth of Jesus
4. The Presentation of Jesus in the Temple
5. The Finding of Jesus in the Temple

Sorrowful Mysteries
(Tuesday and Friday)
1. The Agony in the Garden
2. The Scourging at the Pillar
3. The Crowning with Thorns
4. The Carrying of the Cross
5. The Crucifixion

Glorious Mysteries
(Wednesday and Sunday)
1. The Resurrection
2. The Ascension
3. The Coming of the Holy Spirit on the Apostles
4. The Assumption of Mary into Heaven
5. The Crowning of Mary as Queen of Heaven

The Luminous Mysteries
(Thursday)
1. The Baptism of Jesus
2. The Miracle at Cana
3. Jesus Proclaims the Kingdom of God
4. The Transfiguration of Jesus
5. The Institution of the Eucharist

Praying for those whom you love and those who love and support you is easy. Praying for your former spouse and those affected by your divorce can be challenging and, at times, seems to be impossible. Praying through this difficulty can be a sign of healing and forgiveness. Trust in God's mercy as you reflect on the following people and their intentions while each decade is prayed.

Decade 1: I pray for my child/children.

Decade 2: I pray for my former spouse/partner.

Decade 3: I pray for family and friends whom I have lost because of my divorce.

Decade 4: I pray for my friends (and new relationship/spouse).

Decade 5: I pray for my needs and intentions.

The Divine Mercy Chaplet

"I saw a great light, with God the Father in the midst of it.

Between this light and the earth I saw Jesus nailed to the Cross

and in such a way that God, wanting to look upon the earth, had to look through Our Lord's wounds,

and I understood that God blessed the earth for the sake of Jesus."

— Saint Faustina

1. Using your rosary, begin with the Sign of the Cross, one Our Father, one Hail Mary, and the Apostles Creed.
2. Then, on the Our Father Beads, say the following: Eternal Father, I offer You the Body and Blood, Soul and Divinity of Your dearly beloved Son, Our Lord Jesus Christ, in atonement for our sins and those of the whole world.
3. On the 10 Hail Mary Beads say the following: For the sake of his sorrowful passion, have mercy on us and on the whole world.
   (Repeat steps 2 and 3 for all five decades).
4. Conclude with *(three times)*:
   Holy God, Holy Mighty One, Holy Immortal One, have mercy on us and on the whole world.

Appealing to God for mercy is a way to turn from our sins and let him embrace us in his love. When you feel overwhelmed by guilt pray this prayer for the grace of freedom.

Pope Francis's Prayer to Our Lady Undoer of Knots

"Let the risen Jesus enter your life; welcome him as a friend, with trust: he is life!"
— *Pope Francis, Easter Vigil Homily, March 30, 2013*

Holy Mary, full of God's presence during the days of your life, you accepted with full humility the Father's will, and the Devil was never capable to tie you around with his confusion. Once with your son you interceded for our difficulties, and, full of kindness and patience, you gave us example of how to untie the knots of our life. And by remaining forever Our Mother, you put in order, and make more clear, the ties that link us to the Lord.

Holy Mother, Mother of God, and our Mother, to you, who untie with motherly heart the knots of our life, we pray to you to receive in your hands [the name of whom you are praying for], and to free him/her of the knots and confusion with which our enemy attacks. Through your grace, your intercession, and your example, deliver us from all evil, Our Lady, and untie the knots that prevent us from being united with God, so that we, free from sin and error, may find him in all things, may have our hearts placed in him, and may serve him always in our brothers and sisters. Amen.

What is the one "knot" in your life that causes you the most worry and heartache? Are you willing to allow Mary to help you find solutions?

Psalms

"Still today the Old Testament Book of Psalms gives great power for faith and life. This is simply because it preserves a conceptually rich language about God and our relationships to him. If you bury yourself in Psalms, you emerge knowing God and understanding life."

— *Dallas Willard*

Psalm 51 (For repentance)

Have mercy on me, God, in accord with your
    merciful love;
in your abundant compassion blot out my
    transgressions.
Thoroughly wash away my guilt;
and from my sin cleanse me.

For I know my transgressions;
my sin is always before me.
Against you, you alone have I sinned;
I have done what is evil in your eyes
So that you are just in your word,
and without reproach in your judgment.

Behold, I was born in guilt,
in sin my mother conceived me.
Behold, you desire true sincerity;
and secretly you teach me wisdom.

Cleanse me with hyssop, that I may be pure;
wash me, and I will be whiter than snow.
You will let me hear gladness and joy;
the bones you have crushed will rejoice.

Turn away your face from my sins;
blot out all my iniquities.
A clean heart create for me, God;
renew within me a steadfast spirit.

Do not drive me from before your face,
nor take from me your holy spirit.
Restore to me the gladness of your salvation;
uphold me with a willing spirit.

I will teach the wicked your ways,
that sinners may return to you.
Rescue me from violent bloodshed, God, my
    saving God,
and my tongue will sing joyfully of your justice.

Lord, you will open my lips;
and my mouth will proclaim your praise.
For you do not desire sacrifice or I would give it;
a burnt offering you would not accept.
My sacrifice, O God, is a contrite spirit;
a contrite, humbled heart, O God, you will not scorn.

Psalm 23 (For trust in God)

The LORD is my shepherd;
there is nothing I lack.
In green pastures he makes me lie down;
to still waters he leads me;
he restores my soul.

He guides me along right paths
for the sake of his name.
Even though I walk through the valley of the
    shadow of death,

I will fear no evil, for you are with me;
your rod and your staff comfort me.

You set a table before me
in front of my enemies;
You anoint my head with oil;
my cup overflows.

Indeed, goodness and mercy will pursue me
all the days of my life;
I will dwell in the house of the LORD
for endless days.

Additional Psalms

Psalm 103 (For God's mercy)
Psalm 116 (For thanksgiving)

The Psalms are perfect prayers, inspired by the Holy Spirit. They deal with every aspect of life. They understand the pain of broken relationships, abandonment, grief, and sorrow. They also lift us up when we feel down and cheer us with real joy.

Prayer of Saint John XXIII
for Fathers

"Real fatherhood means love and commitment and sacrifice . . . to share responsibility and not walking away from one's children."

— *William Bennett*

Saint Joseph, guardian of Jesus and chaste husband
of Mary,
you passed your life in loving fulfillment of duty.

You supported the holy family of Nazareth
with the work of your hands.
Kindly protect those who trustingly come to you.
You know their aspirations,
their hardships, their hopes.
They look to you because they know
you will understand and protect them.

You too knew trial, labor, and weariness.
But amid the worries of material life,
your soul was full of deep peace and sang out in
true joy
through intimacy with God's Son entrusted to you
and with Mary, his tender Mother.

Assure those you protect that they do not labor
alone.
Teach them to find Jesus near them and to watch
over him faithfully as you have done. Amen.

Many divorced fathers do not see their children every day. Think about ways you can parent, coach, affirm, and love even from afar.

Litany to Saint Joseph, Patron Saint of Fathers

"How does Joseph exercise his role as protector? Discreetly, humbly, and silently, but with an unfailing presence and utter fidelity, even when he finds it hard to understand."

— Pope Francis, Homily, March 19, 2013

Lord, have mercy.	Lord, have mercy.
Christ, have mercy.	Christ, have mercy.
Lord, have mercy.	Lord, have mercy.
Good Saint Joseph,	pray for us.
Descendant of the House of David,	pray for us.
Husband of Mary,	pray for us.
Foster father of Jesus,	pray for us.
Guardian of Christ,	pray for us.
Support of the Holy Family,	pray for us.
Model of workers,	pray for us.
Example to parents,	pray for us.
Comfort of the dying,	pray for us.
Provider of food to the hungry,	pray for us.
Companion of the poor,	pray for us.
Protector of the Church,	pray for us.

Merciful God, grant that we may learn from Saint Joseph to care for the members of our families and share what we have with the poor.
We ask this through Christ our Lord. Amen.

Turn to Saint Joseph for strength and courage. Pray this litany when you feel alone or when you think you are failing as a father. Saint Joseph will lift you up.

Te Deum (Prayer of Thanksgiving)

"Thankfulness is the beginning of gratitude. Gratitude is the completion of thankfulness. Thankfulness may consist merely of words. Gratitude is shown in acts."

— Henri Frederic Amiel

You are God: we praise you;
You are the Lord: we acclaim you;
You are the eternal Father:
All creation worships you.

To you all angels, all the powers of heaven,
Cherubim and seraphim, sing in endless praise:
Holy, holy, holy Lord, God of
power and might, heaven and earth are full of your
glory.

The glorious company of apostles praise you.
The noble fellowship of prophets praise you.
The white-robed army of martyrs praise you.

Throughout the world the holy Church acclaims
you:
Father, of majesty unbounded,
your true and only Son, worthy of all worship,
and the Holy Spirit, advocate and guide.

You, Christ, are the king of glory,
the eternal Son of the Father.
When you became man to set us free
you did not spurn the Virgin's womb.

You overcame the sting of death,
and opened the kingdom of heaven to all believers.

You are seated at God's right hand in glory.
We believe that you will come, and be our judge.

Come then, Lord, and help your people,
bought with the price of your own blood,
and bring us with your saints
to glory everlasting.
　　　　　— International Consultation on English Texts,
　　　　　　　　　The Liturgy of the Hours, 1975

In any divorce or separation, it is easy to focus on the negative events that have taken place. Pray this prayer of thanksgiving as a way to thank God for all that is good in your life, even when it is difficult to see it.

Act of Faith, Hope, and Love

"So faith, hope, love remain, these three; but the greatest of these is love."

— *1 Corinthians 13:13*

My God, I believe in you,
I hope and trust in you,
I love you above all things,
with all my heart and mind and strength.
I love you because you are supremely good and
worth loving;
and because I love you,
I am sorry with all my heart for offending you.
Lord, have mercy on me, a sinner.
Amen.

Faith, hope, and love are gifts from God. Reflect on ways you can use these gifts in your life.

Act of Contrition

"Thoroughly wash away my guilt;
and from my sin cleanse me."

— *Psalms 51:4*

My God, I am sorry for my sins
with all my heart.
In choosing to do wrong and failing to do good,
I have sinned against you
whom I should love above all things.
I firmly intend, with your help,
to do penance, to sin no more,
and to avoid whatever leads me to sin.
Our Savior Jesus Christ
suffered and died for us.
In his name, my God, have mercy.

— *Rite of Penance*

Do you believe that God can forgive your sins? Can
you forgive yourself? Pray for the ability to be con-
trite, seek God's forgiveness, and forgive yourself as
well.

Part IV: *Personal Prayers and Reflections*

"Whenever we want to ask some favor of a powerful man, we do it humbly and respect-fully, for fear of presumption. How much more important then to lay our petitions before the Lord God of all things with the utmost humility and sincere devotion. We must know that God regards our purity of heart and tears of compunction, not our many words."

— *Saint Benedict*

For Patience

"No one is more patient than God the Father; no one understands and knows how to wait as much as he does."

— *Pope Francis, May 2, 2014 (from a tweet)*

Help me, Lord, to be patient when I am frustrated
   or disappointed,
Long-suffering when I am feeling sad or angry,
Hopeful when I am lonely or in grief.
May I bear my crosses, be they big or small,
   with the aid of your love and grace.
Let me never fall into bitterness or become short-
   tempered with the people around me.
Help me to live with the realization that life on
   earth is brief and my true home is heaven.
Grant that when I must wait for something,
   especially for answers to prayer, that I rest in
   confidence and trust of your love, knowing that
   the right answer will come in your time.
Finally, let me be a blessing to all who come in
   contact with me, especially my family. I ask this
   in the name of the Father, Son, and Holy Spirit.
   Amen.

Saint Francis de Sales said, "Have patience with all things, but first of all with yourself." In what ways and in what situations do I need to be patient and place my trust in God?

For Humility

"I am in competition with no one. I have no desire to play the game of being better than anyone. I am simply trying to be better than the person I was yesterday."

— *Unknown*

O My Jesus!
Remove from me the fear:
That my children love their other parent more,
That they have more fun with their other parent,
That they prefer to be with their other parent

Give me the wisdom to:
Not be jealous of my children's relationship with their other parent,
Not feel competitive with my former spouse,
Not want to be the "favorite" parent.

Give me the grace:
To accept my children's relationship with my former spouse,
To encourage healthy interactions between my former spouse and my children,
To accept that my children can and should love both parents.

O My Jesus, help me be a witness of love to both my children and my former spouse.

Do you act as if you were competing for your child's affection or attention? Pray to be humble and for the ability to accept that your children can and should have a healthy relationship with both of their parents.

For Courage

"You gain strength, courage, and confidence by every experience in which you really stop to look fear in the face. You are able to say to yourself, 'I lived through this horror. I can take the next thing that comes along.'"

— *Eleanor Roosevelt*

Holy Spirit, giver of life and source of strength, when I look into the future, I feel anxious and fearful. I am afraid of what will happen to me and to my children as we go through all these changes in our lives.

It is only when I stop and realize that the only day I have to get through is today and that you have promised to be with me every day of my life that I have the courage to go on.

Help me to trust that you will be with me this moment, and the next and the next. When I feel like giving up or when I fall into despair, grant me your peace and help me to call upon you whenever I am in need — no matter how often that may be — because you are always there, waiting to assist me in my time of trouble. Amen.

Do you feel like giving up? Do you think that your situation will never improve? Trust in God and know that he will give you the courage, strength, and confidence that you need.

For Dealing with Adversity

"There is no evil to be faced that Christ does not face with us. There is no enemy that Christ has not already conquered. There is no cross to bear that Christ has not already borne for us, and does not now bear with us."

— *Pope Saint John Paul II*

Lord Jesus, in the Garden you prayed to the
    Father, "Your will, not mine." Let your prayer
    be my prayer as well in this time of trouble and
    adversity. May I always remember that nothing
    happens to me without your knowledge. May I
    find joy and peace in you, no matter what I am
    going through.
Help me grow in love and charity, knowing that
    you will work all things for good for those who
    love you. Amen.

---

*Do you see the hand of God in all that befalls you?
Read Psalms 31:1-6 and know that God is with you
in times of adversity.*

For Healing

"Healing doesn't mean the damage never existed. It means the damage no longer controls your life."
— *Akshay Dubey*

Dear Lord,
You are the source and giver of life. In you and through you comes all healing.
I put my trust in you, knowing that no one who sought your healing power was left unaided.
I give you my deepest pains and hurts from my divorce, believing that through your Holy Spirit I can be restored to full mental, physical, and emotional health.
I put my trust that you will cleanse me and make me whole again,
able to live fully in the light of the Kingdom and the hope of salvation.
I believe that you love me and want the best for me.
Hear, Oh Lord, my cry, and answer me. Amen.

In what ways do you need to be healed? Reflect on the passion of Christ, and know that he suffers with you through your pain. And reflect, too, on the way he healed all those who came to him, even in the midst of his own suffering.

For Letting Go

"You can't start the next chapter of your life if you keep rereading the last one."

— Unknown

I confess to you, almighty God
that I have greatly sinned.
I ask you to forgive me for all that I have done in
my thoughts and in my words,
in what I have done and what I have failed to do.
Dear God, help me to believe that my desire to
please you does indeed please you and allow me
to feel your forgiveness.
Remove all false guilt from my thoughts and help
me to leave the past in the past.
Enable me to let go of all that no longer helps me
serve you so that I may approach today and
every day as the beginning of a holy, happy and
future life in you. Amen.

---

*Pope Francis has said, "Never let the past determine
your life ... always look forward." Pray for the ability
to let go of past mistakes or sins. Free yourself of guilt,
or of what could have been. Learn from the past, but
live in the present.*

For Peace

"Do not lose your inner peace for anything whatso-
ever, not even if your whole world seems upset. If you
find that you have wandered away from the shelter of
God, lead your heart back to him quietly and simply."
— *Saint Francis de Sales*

Dearest Jesus,
You promised to give us peace.
I come now in need of your peace, the peace that
    passes all understanding.
I am like a child in its mother's arms, needing to
    feel safe and protected.
Whenever I am tempted to worry or fear, draw me
    back into your loving embrace.
Hold me close. Shelter me within your Sacred
    Heart, so that the storms of life cannot destroy
    me.
Let me rest, secure in your love, now and all the
    days of my life.

Jesus said, "Peace I leave with you; my peace I give to
you" (Jn 14:27). What causes you to lose your inner
peace? How can you allow the peace of Jesus to take
precedence in your life?

For Ending Gossip
and the Sin of Detraction

"Gossip can also kill, because it kills the reputation of the person! It is so terrible to gossip! At first it may seem like a nice thing, even amusing, like enjoying a candy. But in the end, it fills the heart with bitterness, and even poisons us. What I am telling you is true. I am convinced that if each one of us decided to avoid gossiping, we would eventually become holy!"

— *Pope Francis, Angelus, February 16, 2014*

God, I know that people are curious about what
    happened between my former spouse and me.
    I know, too, that I often want to be sure that
    everyone knows "my" side of the story.
I realize that this kind of talk is not helpful for my
    healing or the healing of my former spouse or
    children.
Guard me from the temptation to talk too much
    about my situation, and help me to say only
    kind words about my former spouse.
"Do not let any unwholesome talk come out
    of your mouths, but only what is helpful for
    building others up according to their needs, that
    it may benefit those who listen" (Eph 4:29, NIV).

People will talk about your separation and divorce. Some thrive on the misfortune of others. Some may go out of their way to share intimate details of your experience. Pray for them, and pray that you do not contribute to the negativity that may surround you.

For My Former Spouse/Partner

"We all lose somebody we care about and want to find some comforting way of dealing with it, something that will give us a little closure, a little peace."

— *Mitch Albom*

Jesus, I ask you to bless (insert name).
End any feelings of hate and anger between us.
Help me to forgive him/her.
Help me to remember that she/he is probably
    hurting, too.
Most of all, help me to remember that no matter
    what has happened between us, you still love
    both of us.
Be with us and grant us your salvation.

Blessed Teresa of Calcutta said that the only way we can be at peace is through love. End any hate that may exist between you and your former spouse by praying for them.

For Closure of My Past Marriage/ Relationship

"In every friendship hearts grow and entwine them-selves together, so that the two hearts seem to make only one heart with only a common thought. That is why separation is so painful; it is not so much two hearts separating, but one being torn asunder."
— *Venerable Archbishop Fulton Sheen*

Oh Lord, my former spouse and I have been unable to honor the commitment we made on our wedding day.

I pray that you give us the courage and strength to recognize that we can no longer be together as "one flesh," but must separate.

I place myself, my former spouse, and our broken marriage into your hands.

If it is possible that our relationship be restored, I give you thanks.

However, if it is not possible for restoration, then help us both pass through this time of trial with dignity, mutual respect, and kindness so that we do not continue to hurt one another, but instead help one another heal and grow in your love.

One cannot move on if he or she lives in the past. This is one of the most challenging aspects of a divorce. How can you accept that your relationship with your former spouse is over? Pray for the ability to overcome the temptation to replay "what could have been" and focus on the here and now.

For Forgiveness of Self

"Chronic remorse, as all the moralists are agreed, is a most undesirable sentiment. If you have behaved badly, repent, make what amends you can, and address yourself to the task of behaving better next time. On no account brood over your wrongdoing. Rolling in the muck is not the best way of getting clean."

— *Aldous Huxley*

Father, I have asked your forgiveness for the sins
I have committed with regard to my former
marriage. Now I come before you, asking that
you help me forgive myself.
I keep blaming myself for all that I did wrong.
I keep replaying all the things that happened, and I
keep subjecting myself to the pain of memory.
So now I ask that you help me know that because
you have forgiven me,
I can forgive myself for all that I have done and all
I have failed to do.
Let me see myself through your eyes and allow me
to make a new beginning and a fresh start to my
life.

Read Psalms 32:1-7. As you seek God's forgiveness, pray for the ability to forgive yourself as well.

For My New Relationship/Spouse

"What we wait around a lifetime for with one person, we can find in a moment with someone else."

— Stephanie Klein

Thank you, Lord, for bringing a new love and new hope into my life.

I am grateful for this chance to start over.

I never thought I would be so happy again.

I don't want to make the same mistakes this time, so grant me the self-awareness to see where my own fears and issues contributed to the failure of my former relationship.

Help me to root these out of my life so that I can enter into this new relationship with joy and peace.

Bless this relationship, Lord, and make it a sign of your loving presence in the world. Amen.

You may be thinking: "Is this the right person for me? Will I be hurt again? Can I trust again?" Give thanks to God for all things new in your life. Pray that you can let go of past patterns or fears and start your relationship anew.

For Overcoming Difficult Times

"To live by faith means to put our lives in the hands of God, especially in our most difficult moments."

— *Pope Francis, May 23, 2014 (from a tweet)*

Jesus, you are the Light of the World.
We know that you are the Good News of love and
    hope in our lives.
We know that your light and love will get us
    through any difficult and dark times.
Be with us. In your name we pray. Amen.

You may be thinking: "Will this ever end? Will my former spouse ever stop trying to hurt me? I can't take any more!" Put your trust in Jesus and know that he will calm the storms of your life just as he calmed the sea.

For Overcoming Hate

"Hate: It has caused a lot of problems in this world, but it has not solved one yet."

— Maya Angelou

Father, the ending of my marriage has created such pain, such anger between my former spouse and me. It almost feels like the love we once shared has been replaced by hate.

I don't want to live this way.

Send your Spirit, the Consoler, the Source of Holiness

so that bitterness may be replaced with the sweetness of your presence,

anger may be transformed by the joy of your presence,

and hatred may be conquered by the light of your love.

I am yours, Father, now and for always.

Pope Saint John Paul II said, "Darkness can only be scattered by light, hatred can only be conquered by love." What can you do to end bitterness and hatred as a result of your divorce or separation? Pray for the grace to overcome any hostility that may be directed toward you.

For Trust

"Trust is the glue of life. It's the most essential ingredient in effective communication. It's the foundational principle that holds all relationships."

— *Stephen R. Covey*

When my heart is broken ... Jesus, I trust in you.
When anger threatens to destroy my peace ...
    Jesus, I trust in you.
When it feels like my whole world is broken and
    shattered ... Jesus, I trust in you.
When my way is dark and my path is lost ... Jesus,
    I trust in you.
When I am afraid to risk loving ... Jesus, I trust in
    you.
When I don't believe I can ever trust again ...
    Jesus, I trust in you.

Pray the Divine Mercy Chaplet. Place your trust in Jesus. (See Page 41.)

For Hope

"Christ doesn't promise life will be 'a party.' He promises hope — a light at the end of the tunnel."

— Pope Francis, May 30, 2014 (from a tweet)

Jesus, my Savior,

The night of my sorrow is long. It feels as if there will never be a sunrise.

I have no place to turn, no one who can help but you, my Jesus.

I need to be able to hope that things will get better.

I need to be able to hope for a brighter tomorrow.

I need to be able to hope for a happier future.

I need to be able to hope that love will be mine again.

Fill me, Lord, with your hope, so that even in the midst of the dark night of my soul I can know that joy approaches and rejoice in its coming.

In your name I pray, Amen.

Reflect on the quote from Pope Francis. Know that even in your darkest moments Christ will be your light.

For Help and Healing During the Divorce and Annulment Process

"There is another sadness: the sadness that comes to all of us when we take the wrong road.... Be courageous in suffering and remember that after the Lord will come, after joy will come, after the dark comes the sun."

— *Pope Francis, Homily, May 30, 2014*

How long, O Lord, how long must I wait?
Again and again, I think that I've reached the end,
    but then I must wait some more.
Wait for the divorce to be final.
Wait for an annulment.
Wait for a new relationship.
I feel like I'm waiting my life away.
Grant me patience, Lord, so that this time of
    waiting can be a time of healing, a time of
    restoration.
I believe that, through your mercy,
the pain I am feeling will be transformed in the fire
    of your love.
I thank you now for the answers that will come in
    time — your time — and for the healing that is
    coming for me and for those whom I love.

Overcoming the initial pain of replaying what went wrong in your marriage will lead to healing. Pray for patience as you seek a divorce and/or an annulment. Know that over time you will heal from the pain, and trust in God's mercy and love.

For Those I've Lost and Who Have Been Hurt through My Separation/Divorce

"You have taken from me my closest friends
and have made me repulsive to them.
I am confined and cannot escape;
my eyes are dim with grief."

— *Psalms 88:9, NIV*

Jesus, you know what it feels like to be betrayed by
someone you loved.
In my divorce, some of those who I believed to be
my friends have chosen sides and abandoned me.
Even some members of my own family have
rejected me.
The loss of those relationships has created even
more pain in my life.
Help me not to become angry or bitter, but to continue to love even those who no longer love me.
Help us build a new relationship, if that is possible.
If we cannot continue in charity and friendship,
then bless them and keep them in your
everlasting mercy. Amen.

---

*The casualty of most divorces is that you lose friends
and even family members along the way. Have you
caused them pain? What can you do to restore these
relationships? If it is impossible, or if they refuse to
discuss it with you, pray for them. Perhaps over time,
and through prayer, things will change.*

A Prayer for Grandparents

"Divorce affects everyone ... we all know it does and it may be well to remember grandparents in this now stormy lake."

— *Natasha Brittan*

Lord, when my former spouse and I divorced,
  I didn't realize how much it would affect my
  children and their grandparents. Lord, help
  our parents forgive me and my former spouse
  for our broken relationship. And remove
  all obstacles to their having continuing
  relationships with our children. And may they
  be freed of attitudes that might negatively affect
  the children.

Grandparents suffer from divorce, too. They can be caught in the middle between their child and his or her former spouse. A parent with primary custody can be tempted to prevent their former in-laws from being a part of their child's life. What can you do to keep all of your child's grandparents in his or her life?

Part V: *Prayers for the Intercession of the Patron Saints of the Separated/Divorced*

Saint Helena (c. 250–c. 330)

Saint Helena was the mother of Emperor Constantine the Great. When her son was in his teens, her husband, Constantius, divorced her to marry a younger, wealthier woman. At the age of nearly 80, Helena traveled to Jerusalem where she is said to have found the relics of the Cross of Christ. She is often invoked as the patron saint of divorced people.

Holy and blessed Saint Helena,

You know the pain of having been set aside for another person. You know the shame and anguish that comes with divorce, as well as the painful realization that your marriage can never be restored.

Pray for me that I might accept the cross of my divorce with the same grace and charity you accepted your own.

Lead me as I create a new life for myself, that through your intercession I can serve the Lord today and all the days of my life.

Divorce did not prevent Saint Helena from living a committed Christian life and working with her son to honor the holy places of Palestine by sponsoring the construction of churches. Like her, we must accept the grace to move on in our Christian lives and perform the services God calls us to.

Saint Fabiola (d. 399)

Saint Fabiola, a member of a noble Roman family, was a close associate of Saint Jerome. Her first husband was so abusive even Saint Jerome didn't blame her for divorcing him. When she married a second time, against Church teaching, she continued in her faith even though she had to abstain from the sacraments. Upon the death of her second husband, she did penance and returned to full communion with the Church. She is a patron of divorced people and those in abusive marriages.

Saint Fabiola,

I come to you because you understand what it
    is like to have made the decision to remarry
    outside the church and, therefore, not be able
    to receive Communion. Your example of love
    for your second husband while still respecting
    Church teaching encourages me to do the
    same. Help me to continue in my faith, while
    accepting the consequences of my decision to
    remarry. Most of all, Saint Fabiola, never let my
    actions be a cause of scandal to others.

Reflect on Saint Fabiola's courage, obedience, and service. When she remarried after her divorce, she obeyed the discipline of the Church. Only when her second husband died was she restored to full communion. Then she used her riches and time to serve the sick and poor.

Saint Rita (1381–1457)

Saint Rita of Cascia was married at age 12 to a cruel and abusive man. Eighteen years later, when he was killed in a blood feud, she prayed that her sons would die rather than avenge his death. Her prayers were apparently answered when her boys died of dysentery. She is called upon as a patron of those in difficult marriages as well as hopeless cases.

Holy patroness of those in need, Saint Rita, you were humble, pure and patient. Your pleadings with your divine Spouse are irresistible, so please obtain for me from our risen Jesus the request I make of you: [mention your petition]. Be kind to me for the greater glory of God and I shall honor you and sing your praises forever. Glorious Saint Rita, you miraculously participated in the sorrowful passion of our Lord Jesus Christ. Obtain for me now the grace to suffer with resignation the troubles of this life, and protect me in all my needs. Amen.

In the midst of all that is going on because of separation or divorce, imitate Saint Rita's devotion to God in prayer. Decide on a time and regular place to spend time praying daily.

Saint Guntramnus (524–592)

Saint Guntramnus was a sixth-century King of Burgundy. He was married for a time to a woman named Mercatrude, whom he eventually divorced. When she fell ill and her physician failed to cure her, he had the doctor executed. After his conversion to Christianity, he deeply repented of both the divorce and the murder order, spending much time in prayer and penance. He is a patron of divorced people.

Saint Guntramnus,

When you realized the sin of your divorce, you sought forgiveness and did penance. Help me as I struggle with the realization of what my divorce means to me and my family. Intercede for me that I might come to a place of peace as you did and help me not to fall into sin again. I ask this in the name of our Lord Jesus Christ, who reigns now and forever. Amen.

Reflect on Saint Guntramnus's repentance. When you acknowledge some wrongdoing, show your change of heart by performing a simple act of service.

Saint Eugene de Mazenod
(1782–1861)

*Saint Eugene is the unofficial patron of children of
divorced parents. He was a member of the French
nobility. His mother was wealthy, but his father was
poor. The marriage of his parents was deeply troubled,
and eventually his mother divorced his father, leaving Eugene to live alone with his father. His mother
reconnected with him when he was in his twenties,
hoping to marry him to a rich heiress, but he entered
the seminary instead.*

Saint Eugene,
You know what it is like to be a child whose
    parents are divorced. With your aid, help my
    children see the love of Jesus in all my actions
    toward them and toward their other parents.
May God, through your intercession, guide me to
    accept the difficulties that arise from my divorce
    and help me work toward a happy and holy
    solution.
May I accept God's will for my life with strength
    and love, and may I always show God's love to
    my children. I ask this through His Son Jesus
    Christ. Amen.

---

*Pray and think about each of your children and
identify as best you can the effect divorce has had on
them. Look for gentle and affectionate ways to help
and encourage them.*

About the Authors

Woodeene Koenig-Bricker is an author and editor with more than twenty years experience writing for the Catholic press. She was the founding editor of Catholic Parent *magazine and is the author of seven books on saints and spirituality including* 365 Saints *and* Facing Adversity with Grace.

David Dziena holds an M.A. in Pastoral Theology from St. Joseph College and has worked in catechetical ministry for over twenty years. He is a parish acquisitions editor at Our Sunday Visitor. David is also a contributing writer of Faith Fusion: Knowing, Loving, and Serving Christ in the Catholic Church.